# THE TUDORS

Brian Moses is a poet, editor and percussionist who lives on the Sussex coast with his wife and two daughters. He travels the country presenting his poems in schools and libraries. His knowledge of history is extensive and he can say that almost every thing you read in this book might well have been true!

Mike Phillips is big, bald and blooming good fun. He lives in Essex with his wife and three children, illustrating books from his garden shed.

# Hysterical HISTORICAL Poems

# THE TUDORS

Chosen by Brian Moses

Illustrated by Mike Phillips

MACMILLAN CHILDREN'S BOOKS

First published 2000
by Macmillan Children's Books
a division of Macmillan Publishers Ltd
25 Eccleston Place, London SW1W 9NF
Basingstoke and Oxford
www.macmillan.co.uk

Associated companies throughout the world

ISBN 0 330 37715 9

1 3 5 7 9 8 6 4 2

A CIP catalogue record for this book is available from the British Library.

Printed by Mackays of Chatham plc, Chatham, Kent.

# Contents

**Short Livers**   John Kitching                                    1

**The Tudors**   Clare Bevan                                        2

**King Henry VIII**   Andrew Collett                                4

**Henry the Eighth**   Roger Stevens                                7

**Jack the Jester**   David Harmer                                  8

**Head Start**   Trevor Harvey                                     10

**Closing the Monasteries Rap**   John Coldwell                    13

**Anne Boleyn**   Judith Nicholls                                  14

**A True Likeness?**   Andrea Shavick                              16

**The Grocer's Apprentice**   Roger Stevens                        18

**Guess What?**   Patricia Leighton                                21

**Mind Yer 'Ead**   Brian Grindall                                 22

**Bess's Bath**   Dave Calder                                      25

**Why Elizabeth I Never Married**   John Foster                    26

**Doctor, Doctor**   Clare Bevan                                   29

**Rizzio**   Clare Bevan                                           30

**Mary Queen of Scots**   Clare Bevan                                   33

**Ruff Stuff**   Jane Clarke                                           34

**Match of the Day**   Roger Stevens                                   35

**When News Came to Drake**   Tony Langham                             38

**Look Out, It's the Armada!**   Trevor Harvey                         40

**A French Lieutenant, Witnessing the Defeat of the
Spanish Armada**   Mike Johnson                                        41

**Give Us a Kiss, My Lovely**   Bernard Young                          42

**Mr Shakespeare**   Charles Thomson                                   45

**Still Not Bored with the Bard**   James Carter                       46

**Love Letter from Mary Tudor to Her Husband,
Philip of Spain**   Brian Moses                                        47

**Raleigh and Elizabeth**   Colin West                                 50

**Sir Walter Raleigh**   Roger Stevens                                 52

**Tudors**   Peter Dixon                                               54

# Short Livers

Some Tudor folk
Were rich and haughty.
Quite a few
Were cruel and naughty.

Most of them
Were dead by forty!

*John Kitching*

# The Tudors

Henry the Seventh,
A battling man,
Captured the crown
And the Tudors began.

Henry the Eighth
Was next in the line –
Married six wives,
Loved banquets and wine.

Edward the Sixth
Came after his dad –
King for six years
And a sickly young lad.

Mary the First,
A woman of pride,
Lit lots of bonfires
But very soon died.

Elizabeth R,
(Who was known as Queen Bess)
Reigned many years –
Forty-five, more or less.

With Shakespeare and Drake
She won fortune and fame,
But gave us no children
To carry her name.

So that was the end –
All the Tudors were dead . . .
Then along came the Stuarts
To rule us instead.

*Clare Bevan*

# King Henry VIII

King Henry was taught to hunt
he was taught to dance and sing,
he was taught to do all those things
expected from a King.

He was taught to give out orders
he was taught to plot and scheme,
but all Henry really wanted
was to join a football team.

Which is why he wore big bloomers
those which stuck out to the side,
so a half a dozen football shorts
could be neatly tucked inside.

And why he always changed his wife
without looking for a reason,
except he thought it nice to have
a new wife for each season.

And, finally, why King Henry
liked to make heads roll –
so he could have something round
to kick into a goal!

*Andrew Collett*

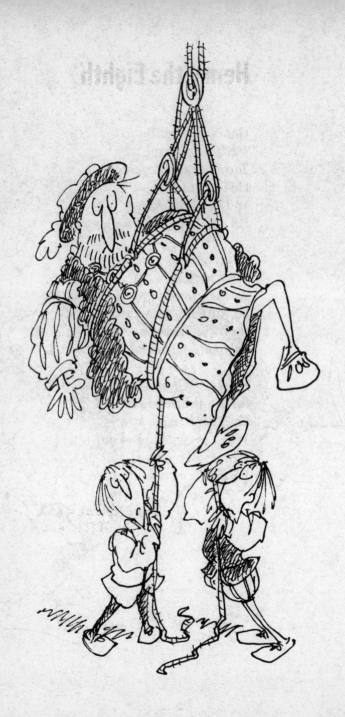

# Henry the Eighth

Henry the Eighth
was a fat old king.
*Tariddle tariddle taree*
He liked to eat
and he liked to sing
*Fol diddle fol diddle fol dee*

I'm too fat to climb
the stairs, he said
*Tariddle tariddle taree*
So with pulleys and ropes
they winched him to bed
*Fol diddle fol diddle fol dee*

He wrote *Greensleeves*
for his girlfriend, 'tis said
*Tariddle tariddle taree*
When his wife found out
He cut off her head
*Fol diddle fol diddle fol dee*

*Roger Stevens*

# Jack the Jester

I'm Jack the jester in my cap and bells
jokes about middens, jokes about smells
jokes about doublets and wrinkled hose
jokes concerning the King's big nose
when you're a jester anything goes.*

I'm Jack the jester with my dog Patch
he does neat tricks, jumps to catch
a tennis ball on his hind legs
barks out numbers, dances, begs
steals my ale and drains the dregs.

I'm Jack the jester, I've lost my grin
you won't believe the mess I'm in
when I told jokes about the Queen
the King got angry, extremely mean
this dungeon is the worst I've seen.

I'm Jack the jester, foolish Jack
it could be thumbscrews or the rack
it was just a laugh, not some plot
but now I'm in a real hot spot
thrown into the Tower to rot.

I'm Jack the jester in better humour
my execution was a rumour
'My little joke,' King Henry said,
'now pick on someone else instead
but don't go mad, don't lose your head!'

*David Harmer*

\*Jack's got that wrong, as this poem shows!

# Head Start

Henry the Eighth lost his heart
To Catherine Howard and Anne Boleyn;
And then, to him, they lost their heads –
'Fair swap,' said Henry with a grin.

(Thus, the very first 'Swap Shop' did begin.)

*Trevor Harvey*

# Closing the Monasteries Rap

Hey everybody – come listen to me
I used to be a monk at Fountains Abbey
Until we got a new king – Henry number eight
Who showed us all the Abbey gate.
Then he took our silver and our gold.
The bells went somewhere never to be tolled
The lead from the roof was taken and sold.
The place became leaky, rotten and holed.
Before long mass destruction starts
They carried off bricks with horse and carts
To build a mansion called Fountains Hall
What once was my home is just a ruin – that's all.

*John Coldwell*

# Anne Boleyn

Would you like to be a queen
with a crown upon your head?
Would you join the king in court,
and share the royal bed?

Would you like to be a queen,
to spread your wit and charm,
with a crown upon your head . . .
and your head beneath your arm?

*Judith Nicholls*

# A True Likeness?

A picture paints a thousand words
But not in Anne of Cleves's case
Henry fell in love with her portrait
But ran off screaming when he saw her face.

*Andrea Shavick*

# The Grocer's Apprentice

Oh, to be an apprentice
Only fifteen and working hard
I wake at dawn, clean up the shop
And wash my hands in the yard.
(*In the summer I wash my feet, too –*
*and I have an all-over bath once a year.*)

Beer and bread for breakfast
Then we open the shop again
Sugar from the Turkish Empire
And pepper stolen from Spain.
(*Those Spaniards don't like to tangle*
*with Francis Drake!*)

I go to bed as darkness falls
Under the counter I sleep
Oh, to be an apprentice
Working six days every week.
(*But I get Sundays and Christmas Day off.*)

There are riots on the streets of London
And everyone has to run
When the Watch is called with their muskets and pikes
But a lad's got to have some fun.
(*There are puppet shows over the river
but Southwark's a real dump.*)

*Roger Stevens*

# Guess What?

Elizabeth Tudor is a swot
Lizzie is teacher's pet
She laps up Latin
Gobbles Greek
She's absolutely wet!

She spouts Italian poetry
Her sums are always right
Her letters are immaculate
Her singing's sweet and light.

Elizabeth T. is a gumboil
Elizabeth T. is a pain
But don't say it aloud.
She may show you the Tower
And you'll never get out again.

*Patricia Leighton*

# Mind Yer 'Ead

I'm an executioner just doin' my job
People always think I'm a bit of a slob,
But underneath this mask I'm a sensitive guy
when I pick me victim's 'ead up
I really could cry
chop chop, chop chop, chop chop.

I visit all me customers the night before,
I say 'it's nuffin personal, it's just the law,'
I tell 'em they'll be fine and they won't feel much,
me axe is like a razor wiv a velvet touch,
chop chop, chop chop, chop chop.

An' now I must confess that I drink too much beer,
It's ruinin' me aim and I can't see so clear,
I just might miss yer neck and cut yer arm 'arf through,
or if I'm really drunk I'll 'ave your fingers too,
chop chop, chop chop, chop chop.

CHOP

*Brian Grindall*

# Bess's Bath

With pails of hot water the ladies in waiting
run up the stairs.
The courtiers sniff at their scented pomanders,
the ambassadors laugh
they think it so weird: for the third time this year
Elizabeth Tudor is taking a bath.

In the royal bedchamber the queen sits in state
in her steamy tub,
she's removed her red wig to rub her head better
with ring-crusted fingers
and scrubbed the white powder from her face to reveal
care-worn wrinkles and smallpox scars.

Through teeth blackened by sugar she starts to whistle
and says in her heart:
I may not have Mary Stewart's looks (or her neck),
but she never sees soap,
and Philip of Spain may be filthy rich, but today
I'm the cleanest monarch in Europe.

*Dave Calder*

# Why Elizabeth I Never Married

She couldn't find a suitor to suit her
Among all her courtiers at court.
As she smoothed down her dress,
She said, 'Well, I guess,
I'm just not the marrying sort.'

*John Foster*

# Doctor, Doctor

Hot and sweaty?
Buy my leeches.
Fade your freckles
With my bleaches,
Growing wrinkles?
Turning bald?
Slap on grease
Congealed and cold.
Nasty headache?
Just can't cope?
Try a touch of
Hangman's rope.
Gran's gone deaf?
Use vixen's lard.
Children fretful?
Beat them. Hard.
Scared of fevers?
Sick of spells?
My pomanders
Hide the smells.
Skin all spotty?
Feeling ill?

If the plague doesn't get you
My medicines will!

*Clare Bevan*

# Rizzio

**(Mary Queen of Scots Mourns
for Her Murdered Italian Friend.)**

Rizzio,
O, Rizzio,
They've chopped you
Into chipzzio,
I've almost lost
My witzzio –
And all for one
Small kizzio.

But I shall soon
Be quitzzio ...
I'll blow the brutes
To BITTZZIO!

*Clare Bevan*

# Mary Queen of Scots

When they chopped off her head
At Old Fotheringay
There were rumours and stories
And new games to play.

There were songs about seashells
And maids in a row,
There were tales of a wig
Where her hair used to grow.

There were people who spoke
Of a dog, weak and small,
Who hid at her feet
Till it heard the axe fall,

And the blade was too blunt,
And the Queen was too proud,
And her last words of courage
Brought gasps from the crowd,

And some said her beauty
Was nothing but paint,
Some called her a traitor,
Some called her a saint,

But the terrible truth
Of that blood-spattered day
Is locked in the walls
Of Old Fotheringay.

*Clare Bevan*

# Ruff Stuff

Getting hot under the collar?
Are ruffs making you feel rough?
Then starch your ruffs with Ruff Stuff.
Ruff Stuff smoothes rough ruffs.

*Jane Clarke*

# Match of the Day

Welcome listeners
as you join me, Les Dineham,
on Plymouth Ho
for the West Country Bowls Championship.

It's a windy day but the sun is shining
and Sir Francis Drake
is about to throw his first wood.

An expectant hush falls on the small crowd
as Sir Francis lines up the shot.
Look at that smooth arm action
and he swings
and the wood is rolling smoothly towards the jack
easy now
easy
and
Oh, there seems to be a disturbance in the crowd
shouting and waving
the Spanish Armada has been sighted
in the Sound.

Are they going to abandon the game?
No, Sir Francis wants to continue.
He's coolly lining up his second shot
but no one is watching him
Everyone is staring out to sea

The wood rolls slowly along this perfect pitch
easy now
easy

And from my position in the commentary box
I can see the Armada
great tall ships coming over the horizon
The crowd is going frantic

easy now
easy
and the wood is
just nestling against the jack


Sir Francis has won the game!
And now over to Trevor MacDonut
for news of impending invasion.

*Roger Stevens*

# When News Came to Drake

When news came to Drake
About the Spanish Armada,
He said, 'Don't worry lads –
We English are harder!

Let me finish my game,
Then we'll sort them out.
They'll not know what hit them
Once we give them a clout!

We'll teach them a lesson,
They'll never forget.
They think they're the best,
But they've not met us yet.

So we'll send them a message.
This is what it'll say –
INVASION? – FORGET IT.
NO WAY, JOSE!'

*Tony Langham*

# Look Out, It's the Armada!

The cannons fired and – through the air –
The balls come whizzing, rake on rake;
The sailors all bobbed up and down
And shouted 'DUCK!' to Drake.

*Trevor Harvey*

# A French Lieutenant, Witnessing the Defeat of the Spanish Armada

Un
deux
trois
quatre
sank.

*Mike Johnson*

# Give Us a Kiss, My Lovely

**(A Tudor sailor returns home to his sweetheart)**

Your gums are rotten.
Your breath is foul.
You wear a permanent
seafarer's scowl.

*But give us a kiss, my lovely.*

You've lived for months
on salted meat.
You're riddled with disease
from your head to your feet.

*But give us a kiss, my lovely.*

You've chewed on hard biscuits.
You've drunk only ale.
You've gone downhill
since you set sail.

*I have got the scurvy*
*but I am still yours*
*so now that I'm back*
*on these friendly shores*

*Won't you give us a kiss, my lovely?*

Oh, come on then . . . Ugh!
I think it's time you went back to sea.

*Then kiss me goodbye, my lovely.*

Bernard Young

# Mr Shakespeare

I'm Mister Shakespeare.
I pace the stage.
I'm one of the greatest
hits of the age.

My number ones
are *Hamlet* and *Macbeth*.
I like to write
about blood and death.

Murderers lurking,
armies crashing –
stabbing, hacking,
skewering, slashing!

Axe and dagger,
pike and claymore –
this is what
the public pay for!

They're also fond
of booing and hissing
and they like a bit
of slobbery kissing!

*Charles Thomson*

# Still Not Bored with the Bard

That Shakespeare was a clever chap
He wrote a lot of plays –
Some are funny, some are not
And some go on for days

There's always lots of murders
And people in disguise
And royals ranting on about
The meaning of their lives

Though some say Shakespeare never wrote
A poem or a play
But does it really matter?
They're magic anyway!

*James Carter*

# Love Letter from Mary Tudor to Her Husband, Philip of Spain

(Spot the anachronism – an object in its wrong time!)

Dear Philip, my Phil
it's making me ill
to think that
you don't love me.
I love you my dear
but you're making it clear
that this marriage
was not meant to be.

I'm here all alone,
if only you'd phone,
send a pigeon
or simply just write.
Invite me, please do,
Ibiza with you
would soon set
our marriage alight.

Dear Philip, my love,
my sweet turtle dove,
I know it's with you
I relate.
I wish you'd return
and help me to burn
all those plotting
against the state.

Everybody I know
says you should go
but I need you
to give me an heir.
Do you think that I'm neater
than a sweet senorita
or do your eyes
wander elsewhere?

Dear Philip, I'm willing
to share double billing,
if our love could be
re-ignited.
Then our reign as one
will be equal to none,
King and Queen of
two countries united.

So Philip, my Phil
come home, say you will,
without you it's really
quite scary.
Forsake sunny Spain
for the cold English rain
and the arms of
your loving wife, Mary.

xxxxx

*Brian Moses*

# Raleigh and Elizabeth

When Raleigh met Elizabeth,
And it was rather muddy,
He wouldn't let her feet get wet,
He *was* a fuddy-duddy.

So he laid down his velvet cloak,
The Queen, she didn't falter.
She thought it odd, but on it trod,
And said, 'Arise, Sir Walter.'

*Colin West*

# Sir Walter Raleigh

In the Tower of London
where the walls of stone
are as thick as a pharaoh's tomb,
sits Walter Raleigh all alone,
where the ghosts of the Princes
murmur and moan,
and he stares into the gloom.

He dreams of the days
when he travelled the seas
far and wide to exotic shores.
He discovered potatoes,
tobacco to smoke,
and everyone said – What a jolly good bloke,
but they don't say that any more.

They say that he plotted
against Good Queen Bess.
Now his friendship with her
has gone sour.
So he sits and he writes
to pass the time,
and occasionally pens
an amorous rhyme,
condemned for life
in the Tower.

*Roger Stevens*

# Tudors

I've never seen a Tudor
They don't live down our street
I've never seen one walking
I've never heard one speak . . .
I've never ever touched one
They seem so far away
but teacher seems to like them
and we have them every day.

*Peter Dixon*

# Middle Ages

## Poems chosen by Brian Moses

### Career Opportunity: Knight Required

Are you brave, honourable
and chivalrous?
Do you like wearing metal suits
and enjoy being called Sir?
Then this could be the job for you.

Your duties will include
wielding a sword, jousting
and clanking about.

Preference will be given
to those candidates
who come equipped
with their own warhorse and squire.

*Bernard Young*

# Hysterical Historical Poems

# The Romans

## Poems chosen by Brian Moses

### It Could Have Been Reme

Romulus argued
with Remus, his brother,
about where to build Rome,
one hill or the other.
Neither gave way.
Bad-tempered, strong-willed,
they fought one another,
and Remus was killed.
Romulus gloated.
"How sad. It would seem
they'll be calling it Rome.
But it could have been Reme!"

*Marian Swinger*

# The Victorians

**Poems chosen by Brian Moses**

### Victorian Inventors

Wellington had Wellingtons
Rowland had his stamps
Brunel – he had his bridges
and Davey – Davey lamps
There was Lister's Auntie Septic
Penny's Farthing Bikes
. . . but best of all Lord Sandwich
The one we always like!

*Peter Dixon*

# A selected list of poetry books available from Macmillan

The prices shown below are correct at the time of going to press. However, Macmillan Publishers reserve the right to show new retail prices on covers which may differ from those previously advertised.

---

| | |
|---|---|
| **Hysterical Historical Poems: Victorians** | 0 330 37713 2 |
| Poems chosen by Brian Moses | £2.99 |
| | |
| **Hysterical Historical Poems: Middle Ages** | 0 330 37714 0 |
| Poems chosen by Brian Moses | £2.99 |
| | |
| **Hysterical Historical Poems: Tudors** | 0 330 37715 9 |
| Poems chosen by Brian Moses | £2.99 |
| | |
| **Hysterical Historical Poems: Romans** | 0 330 37716 7 |
| Poems chosen by Brian Moses | £2.99 |
| | |
| **A Seacreature Ate My Teacher** | 0 330 39064 3 |
| Poems chosen by Brian Moses | £2.99 |
| | |
| **Aliens Stole My Underpants** | 0 330 34995 3 |
| Poems chosen by Brian Moses | £2.99 |

---

All Macmillan titles can be ordered at your local bookshop or are available by post from:

**Book Service by Post**
**PO Box 29, Douglas, Isle of Man IM99 1BQ**

Credit cards accepted. For details:
Telephone: 01624 675137
Fax: 01624 670923
E-mail: bookshop@enterprise.net

**Free postage and packing in the UK.**
Overseas customers: add £1 per book (paperback)
and £3 per book (hardback)